# The Ar

Samuel Webb

BookLeaf
Publishing

India | USA | UK

Presentation by *BookLeaf Publishing*

Web: www.bookleafpub.com

E-mail: info@bookleafpub.com


ISBN: 9789358313208

First edition 2024

# DEDICATION

I dedicate this book to the hands that are holding it, the eyes that are reading it, and most of all to the hearts moved by it. I imagine you are few, and this is for you.

# ACKNOWLEDGEMENT

I'd like to thank every poet
For inspiring me
My Family, chosen or otherwise
For supporting me
And my ex
Who kindly gave me free time and
Some new material

# PREFACE

All that blood was never once beautiful, it was just red.
-Kait Rokowski

Red is my favorite color
And fresh blood
Marks the page best
If everything is ruined anyway
Let me make something of
All this
Bloody
Mess

# It's a living..

-So..
What do you do?-

I come when you call
It's 3 a.m. and
every body is awake
expect one
by some cruel miracle
and a good dose of
asphalt fury
my siren call
turns a twenty-minute drive
into ten
Anyone who knows
anything knows
that's ten too long
No ones touched him
But they pay me
to break the ribs
and massage the blood
back into the stubborn meat
Mementos rattle in a china cabinet
The same wailing faces around you
sit also still
framed and smiling

on every wall
A silent audience
from a happier time
I take a reading
Twelve ways from Sunday
Jumper cables charged and ready
I pull the lever
Tamed lightning
adrenaline
and broken ribs
at 3 a.m.
Like a bad dream
where every body is awake
except one
I wipe away the blood sweat and tears
I come when you call
and I'm sorry

# How to [Saying Goodbye]

-Would you please
Hold my hand Stranger
I don't want to be alone with this
I'm not afraid to die
But
Does it have to hurt?
Tell me it's easy
Even if its a lie-

Its okay
Let me tell you
exactly what to do
tell them you're not scared
Even if you are
remind them you love them
Even though they know it
tell them you're sorry for going
Even when you know you have to
because they are brave
and they love you
and they understand
And I'm afraid it does hurt,
and they learn to live with it
without you

# An immortal moment

It's late and
that's okay
We watch the same movie
at the same time
in different states
Sharing two couches at once

I look down at the screen
pretending it's a tiny window

For a moment you're in arms reach
and everything is perfect

Your eyes hold that familiar promise of
I love you
You nod off over time
but I don't hang up
I cradle my phone
and tuck it
into a golden nest of satin sheets

For a moment you're in arms reach
and everything is perfect

# On the wrong side of the phone

I answer the call
I catch two words and
My ears ring themselves numb
I understand the rest without really hearing it
It's a long walk down a short hall
with keys enlaced in a white-knuckle grip and
they fight back
Biting at my palms with a soothing sting
I step into my car and step out again,
except I'm somewhere else
Not much of me is here
There are others but
I don't really see them
I'm looking for you but
you're not here
and I know you never will be again

# Eye contact Ratio

Sensory overload
Quips and comments
Absent minded
A warm seat in a cold room
The after taste of lunch
Deep breaths
Thinking so much
about looking normal
That I don't

-Can I get anyone anything else?-

I'm fine, if everyone else is, thanks
Now where was I..

# Daydream Graveyard

I can conjure
whole worlds to mind
Yet to put them to page is
Elluding
How do I put to paper
What breathes
And dies
A tree falling in an empty wood
My thoughts are haunted with them

# You've changed

The same man cannot enter the same river
Twice
The man is everyone
The river is every
passing
moment
And never seeing them
the same again
Matters

# Townie's Requiem

When's the next crusade
Homecoming King?
Always said you'd never end up staying
You settled down when you had your little girl
Promised that you'd give her your whole world

# Sculpt(or/er)

May we never be what they make of us
May we only ever be
what we've made of ourselves

# How to [Give up]

-I don't know where you're at, but I'm done..-
O.k.
Well
let's give it some time
then
I have things of yours
And
you have things of mine
We will meet when we are ready
and exchange
We're okay
You chose not to be my person
So I'll grow from this and
Become better
Then share that version
With someone else..
I thought
We could grow together and
Become better for each other
But I have been wrong before..

-That was too easy
You don't have to smile-

Were you hoping

To hurt me again?
You
doubting
You
cheating
You
giving up
made it easy
If I have to beg
It's not real

# Don't tell me the odds

I know the odds
I grew up on the wrong side of the odds
So did most of my friends.
The odds are in every movie
There are whole books about the odds
Albums about the odds
I walk the streets every day
Folks walking around
Every where
Beaten down by the odds
But then
I see
An old couple
Sharing a blanket and
Tossing stale crumbs
To doves and crows
Stopping only
To tuck each other in
And I'm reminded
Sometimes
The odds get beaten too
I am not a statistical improbability
I'm a choice

# Star Crosser

I once promised you;
That we were meant to be
and
If our names were not
Already etched intertwined
into the heavens
Galactic braille under god's fingers
Then I would drag
Raging suns
Across a crushing void
Spanning light-years
To cross our stars
Now here I sit
Healing
Under a scattered sky
With two burnt hands

# Sour

Life hands you lemons
Suddenly everybody
Starts calling for lemonade
But I'm still waiting on sugar

# Recollection tax

A time will come where I will be able to think,
"You would have loved this.."
and it will not light a fire in my chest
that leaves ash in my gut
and chokes my throat with smoke

# This game ruins friendships

A decade of
Knowing you
Ends after a year of
Loving you
I'm not sure what I regret most
Falling in love with you
Or losing a friend

# Disgusting habit

Men line the gutters
Next to lipstick stained butts
All lit up
Sucked down
Burnt out
Then tossed aside for the next pack of smoke
Disgusting habit

# SaveOurSouls

If I were bleeding
If I had broken a bone
You'd help me
You'd ask
If I'm alright
If it's been hard.
Now the wound can't be seen
There's no plague or laceration but
I feel weak and
It aches

-Asking can be rude
I'm not a professional
Besides
What can be done..-

I hear you but
Support and well wishes
Never fixed what was broken before
And yet I could use them now
More than ever

# Calhoun's Crowding

Why did we commodify mental health?
shelter?
food?
water?
There's so many suffering
What if..
What if
we won't all fit
and
the powers that be
are calling for a culling
factory streamlined
Infinite proliferation in a dwindling finite space
The rats lose their will to flourish
Mass extinction
by a pay wall
Why did we ever commodify
mental health?

# Head Underwater

-Just breath
You can breath through anything-

What if I'm drowning?

-Then kick, hard,
you look for the light and scramble for it
desperatly.
Then you breathe..-

# I'm very Proud of you..

I see the scrapes on your knees yet
you charge the hill with your Sisyphus smile
Hot wax scorching your back as
you learned to fly without your wings
Despite these impossible challenges of life
here you stand
cloaked in Lion's mane
glowing like the dawn despite the rain
God's were built of weaker stuff

Milton Keynes UK
Ingram Content Group UK Ltd.
UKHW031857170324
439575UK00015B/870